DEAR PARENTS

Strategies to Help Your Loved One Through Addiction.

Jennifer Maneely

Printed in the United States of America
First Edition

ISBN 978-1-7333538-0-9

Maneely Publishing
109 Camp Hill Rd.
Mill Spring, NC. 28756

"If you are holding their wings, they cannot fly."

Jennifer Maneely

Edited by Laura P. Baley

Praise for Dear Parents

"This is the book a parent of an addict turns to when it's clear that more of the same will never be enough, and the desire to do whatever it takes to break free from the pain has never been stronger. It illuminates this choice is taking on an assignment of a lifetime, and the deep-seeded commitment it requires to successfully repair and close the wide rift in this important relationship. Or walk away grounded in the knowledge that the decision to do so is made from an informed place and an act of love." -*Melissa McNair, MCC, MSC*

"This book is wonderful! I loved it. It's the truth, it's raw, personal, and most importantly it shows how much Jen cares about the parents with loved ones in addiction and how they can help their kid." -*Laura P. Baley: Editor*

"Excellent quick read! Gives a starting point for those whose loved ones are suffering from addiction. It gives you permission to focus on YOUR healing and break the bonds of codependency."-Kristin C., M.A., NCC

"If you're looking for a book to tell you that 'Everything is going to be ok,' this is not the book for you. If you're looking for a book to challenge you, help you grow, and push you, then you've found it! Jen provides readers with hope in the form of tough questions, hard truths, and the perfect sprinkling of her own personal experiences. This book is great not only for parents of addicts but really any family member or close friend who has found themselves struggling with how to handle and approach their relationship with an addict." -Morgan Poff, MSC

Contents

FORWARD

Hi, I'm Lynn Carnes, Jen's mom. If you are reading this, you likely have a child in addiction. My heart goes out to you. I've been where you are. Starting with her 22nd birthday, I discovered that Jen was an addict.

She didn't become an addict then. Oh no. That's just when I finally got it. Her addiction had begun many years before. I was blind to it for a long time. Looking back, I have to chuckle at all the signs I missed. Sometimes we really do only see what we want to see.

My behavior as her parent was also a significant part of her addiction, even though I was not the one handing her drugs. What I WAS doing was ignoring signs, being caught up in my own world and just barely surviving my own chaotic life.

Then, through a series of fortunate events and some wake-up calls, I began to change.

My wake-up calls may have saved her life. I know it saved mine.

Thanks to being part of a leadership development program that had a heavy emphasis on self-awareness, an important seed was planted. As I developed self-awareness, my understanding of my part in Jen's addiction became acute. I came to realize several critical things:

1. I could no longer try to rescue her, especially since she was not living under my roof.

2. I could not change her, no matter what incentives I offered, be they money or punishment

3. I needed to breathe

4. She felt justified destroying her life to pay me back for being a less than perfect mom - and if I bought into that story, it would only make things worse

5. She had to own her own life

6. She might die from her addiction

7. My greatest strength would come from prayer

In many ways, the mom who raised Jen (as a single parent) had to grow up to save Jen's life. And mine.

When I did that, I was able to set the conditions for her recovery.

That's what I want you to be able to do: set the conditions for your child's recovery. But always remember, they have to choose it for themselves.

Jen has been helping parents, including my executive coaching clients, do that for many years now. No one understands what is going on in an addict's life better than another addict.

The most important lesson I got in her recovery was this: addicts lie, cheat and manipulate in order to fuel their addiction. As parents, we are overmatched from the start. We cannot imagine the things our little babies will do to get their high.

If we stick to the parenting strategies that worked for our children when they were young, we are doomed from the start.

It's a whole new game and no one prepares us for it. You have to create a whole new relationship with yourself first and then with your child.

If you have reached the point of desperation to read this book, you are in the right place. Jen can help you as she has so many parents before you. I've seen it and heard the stories of success and survival.

You can only do that if you are seeing things as they are, not as you want them to be. You need clear eyes to develop a strategy for dealing with your child. You have to find the places where you have control and let go of those places where you don't. That was maybe my hardest lesson.

The fact that I had to change was both hard to swallow and the biggest reward. My life today is very different... in a good way. The changes I had to make to help Jen own her life are the same ones I needed to make to own MY life.

Grateful doesn't begin to describe the way I feel today. I'm grateful that Jen chose life.

And I'm grateful for the many clear-eyed, strong people that helped guide and encourage me through her recovery.

My hope and prayer is that you find something in this book that works for you - and that no matter what, you reach out for help. There are so many resources available, which Jen shares in this book.

My best to you on your journey. Remember to breathe!

PREFACE

Hi. I'm Jen. I am a recovering addict. My mom and I have been on a long, life-changing, soul-shattering, and heartwarming journey through my addiction into my recovery... Our recovery. I am here to share these very personal experiences with you because I want this for you and your child. I will tell you how I changed, and perhaps more importantly, how *she* changed, which served as the catalyst for the beginning of my road to recovery.

There is an enormous lack of resources for parents seeking help while their child is suffering from addiction. It is my mission to address this problem and help as many parents as I can. Based on our journey and hundreds of hours of research and education, I have developed a proven method that works.

I would never call myself a writer or an author of any kind. I won't pretend the book is perfect with the best writing you've ever seen. I'm simply a person who has sat back and watched thousands of parents go into absolute despair and desperation trying to figure out how they can help. So, I wrote this book to provide parents with the thing they need the most...strategies and hope.

I use foul language in this book. Addiction is not conservative or clean. It's messy and often leaves you with little to say other than bad words and maybe a prayer. I have found that even the most conservative people are left cussing.

I have chosen to focus on the parents specifically because generally speaking, they end up becoming the primary caretakers of the addict with some of the most complicated dynamics that you can have in a relationship AND no matter what happens, you will always be their parent.

In this book, you will read about the Four Stages of Addiction. You will see where your loved one fits, and you will find solutions for each stage. You will read about the Five Areas, where parents, often unknowingly, make the most mistakes that set back the recovery of their child because you are entering into a world that doesn't make sense to you.

And what I mean by using the term "mistakes," it's not about taking responsibility for their addiction as you are absolutely not to blame, it's simply about being the human being you are with many lessons left to learn. I continue to learn my own lessons and gain new insights day in and day out, and so will you.

Imagine going over to a foreign country where you don't speak the language without a guide or interpreter. Addiction follows a different set of rules and speaks a different language. Without a guide or interpreter in a foreign country, mistakes would be made. Without a guide through addiction, mistakes will be made. But should not be shamed.

You will find many "me too" moments throughout this book, and you will nod along. You may get angry, you may cry, then become filled with hope and joy.

In the final two chapters: *What Do I Do Now,* and *Your life will never be the same,* you will find more strategies and more help and left with direction and hope you are looking for. But the most important piece of all is that you will find that you are not alone on this road. I am here to help.

CHAPTER 1

INTRODUCTION

When I was a kid, I never imagined myself shooting up heroin and cocaine, getting chased by drug dealers, being held up at gunpoint, or praying to be thrown in jail just so I knew I wouldn't die, and the lies could finally end.

But I wouldn't take any of it back.

When I was younger, I had a vision of what an addict looked like, smelled like, acted like. I didn't fit into that picture. And because I didn't fit into that picture, it took me a long time to accept that I wasn't just a college kid experimenting with finding themselves. I used that as an excuse for myself long after I could get away with it.

They say hindsight is 20/20. Looking back, I can see all the dynamics that played into me becoming the quintessential drug addict. It wasn't just one event or one struggle that got me there. It was all the combinations of decisions and events that became the reality I created for myself along the way.

Addiction does not discriminate. It does not matter how much money you have, what kind of house you grow up in, if you have good parents, bad parents- it doesn't matter. I've talked to tens of thousands of addicts. I've heard all their stories. We have come from every kind of background you could imagine. We all have our stories, this is mine.

CHAPTER 2

THE BEGINNING: THE CREATION OF MY BELIEF SYSTEM

A common theme that comes up in most stories you hear about addiction is a trauma that took place in the developmental stages of the individual.

I want to be clear about this theme. This is *not* a requirement for becoming an addict. I have personally heard hundreds of stories of addicts who did not have traumatic events in their lives, therefore this is not a deciding factor. For me, I did experience trauma and a lot of what I told myself surrounding the trauma supported an unhealthy belief system that infiltrated my thoughts for years. I believed that I deserved what was coming to me and it was all my fault.

At this point, you are probably wondering what the trauma is. There are two reasons I'm not going to tell you:

1. It's very personal. It's not a secret or anything that I am ashamed of, but it's not useful to share such details in a public forum.

2. Sharing details may cause you to blame all of my problems and issues shared here on this one thing and use it as a way to stay caught up in your own denial. Example: "Well, that didn't happen to my son/daughter so maybe they aren't an addict after all."

The trauma does not define my story. But it did help create a belief system within me. From a young age, I was going to therapy over this traumatic event. I kept getting told, "It's not your fault."

As a child, all I could hear was, "It's all your fault." Have you noticed how kids don't really understand concepts in early development? Generally speaking, a child does not have a firm understanding of concepts until around 11-15 years old.

So, as a 6 or 7-year-old that is getting told it's not my fault, I didn't understand "Not." The belief system that was being created around the trauma was this: I felt as though I had done something wrong, it was all my fault, and I was a bad kid.

Starting with this belief system I created, I will explain how that belief system influenced the creation of my addiction. It all stems around the idea of not feeling smart enough like I don't belong in this world and the overall theme of not being good enough.

When it comes to not feeling smart enough, I have to look at my mom again. This may sound like my mom is the cause of my addiction, and she is not. It was simply the perceptions of my little girl brain that translated a certain reality into Jen's world.

Her way of processing information and mine are very different. She jumps from point A-Z very quickly. Most of the time, she figures the middle part out later. Me on the other hand, I need to know A, B, *and* C, before I ever start something.

I hate ambiguity, she thrives in it. Therefore, as a mom, she would say things like "I need you to get to the point faster or keep up with me."

My kid brain translated this as, "I am slow," and," I am stupid. "No, I'm simply methodical and need to think things all the way through. Now as an adult, I can see where this can be a great asset! It can also come with its own set of complications where I can often find myself stuck. But as a kid with a mom that was always so much faster than her, my belief system was that I am not smart.

I constantly confirmed this by my grades in school, which were poor. But I also didn't try. I would "confirm" many of these belief systems created early on, in many of the situations that happened in my life.

Because I believed I wasn't good enough, every time something bad happened, and every time I acted out in a negative way, I confirmed that belief over and over.

Chapter 3

Concrete Evidence that Something was Wrong with Me

Middle School: Oh boy, the *real* awkward years. The years in which my emotions started blossoming. I wish I could say that my body was blossoming like everyone else's, but that just wasn't my story. We moved a lot, and I had a hard time making friends. Because of my past trauma, trusting people did not come naturally.

Adolescent hormones really started taking their toll around eighth grade, and my emotions seemed to spiral out of control. I tried to get a grip on them, but nothing seemed to work. There were also big changes going on at home. My mom met a man. They were engaged and married fairly quickly. He made it a point to make me a part of all of his decisions, and this was exciting to me! Some changes are good, but they can also be scary. I found myself adjusting to a brand-new way of life at home with my hormones infiltrating every fiber of my being. It just became too much for my middle school brain and body to handle.

I became suicidal. It wasn't that I wanted to die, it's just that I didn't know how to live. And now, with the flood of new emotions coming in, life was becoming a real struggle. It wasn't that I couldn't talk about it. Looking back, I think I was afraid, and I think I just I didn't know I was supposed to talk about it.

I mean, how do you talk about something when you really can't put words to it? I was really starting to get good at shutting things down, and I had NO clue how it was going to affect my life. It's the only thing I knew how to do. I thought if I opened my mouth and was honest, I would get in trouble.

There seemed to be a lot of things I wasn't supposed to do, and I wasn't about to add another to the list. So, I just kept my mouth shut, and told myself it wasn't that big of a deal. How do you know how things are going to affect you years down the line? Was I hiding who I really was? It's not like in middle school my thought process was "Oh, I am a lesbian, better hide that from everyone." I didn't even know what it all meant. Yet.

I had a suicide attempt in eighth grade. That's what they called it, but that's not what it was. I was just so tired. I was tired of dealing and I just needed an escape. I don't think I was ever intending to kill myself, but I put a hodgepodge of pills together and brought them to school. I told my two friends I was going to take them all. It wasn't a big deal; I didn't mean it. My friends stole my pills and reported me to the school. I'm so glad they did.

A lot of things changed that day in eighth grade. Mostly the way people treated me, especially the teachers. I got out of a history test because the teacher didn't want to stress me out.

People treated me differently, and that was a good thing. But in the big picture, I wasn't really facing the things I was struggling with, because I didn't know they were big things I was struggling with at the time.

Although I had no clue yet what I was struggling with, I knew we were getting ready to move again. Good. Fresh start. Private school. Right in the middle of eighth grade.

CHAPTER 4

MY MOTHER: THE RAGING BITCH

Yes, I called my mom a raging bitch. I'm allowed to because I lived through her raging bitch years. She did a TEDxTryon speech called "From Raging Bitch to Engaging Coach." I helped her with her title.

How does a daughter get away with calling her that in this chapter? Mostly because it isn't true anymore. We are able to look back on the years in which she acted like a raging out of control person and acknowledge that this existed and yet, it's not this way anymore.

Does it seem like I'm all over the place so far as you read this book? Good. It's very intentional. Think back to your own childhood. It's often messy and all over the place when you think back on it. And this book isn't meant to be my autobiography, it's meant to give help provide you insights and real strategies to face the hell you are in right now and how to go through it as gracefully and supportive as possible.

Back to the raging bitch.

Almost all of the women on my mom's side of the family have tempers. We lose our minds over the dumbest shit, including myself. To give you an example, let me tell you about my experience with avocado. In my late 20's I discovered I loved avocado and decided I wanted some avocado. However, I had never purchased or prepared an avocado at this point in my life.

I went to the store picked up a couple of pretty green avocados, and I was really excited to get home and eat them. I cut into them and found nothing but green, hard, plastic-like grossness. I was pissed! The store had clearly ripped me off, AND I couldn't enjoy my avocado I was craving. So, I did what any normal, sane person would do, which was throw all that shit on the ground, hard.

As I had my full-blown temper tantrum, I watched it splatter all over the walls in the kitchen. Then, I cut into the second one. I couldn't believe it! The same plasticky phenomenon happened to that damn avocado too! It suffered the same fate as the first one. A few moments later I paused, looked at my avocado covered kitchen, and had a thought. Maybe it was *me?* Could it be that maybe, just *maybe*, I needed to do some research on avocados and their ripening process.

My growing up experience with my mom was similar to the kitchen smeared with smashed avocado. We were in a grocery store. It was the late 80's or early 90's. She wanted strawberries, and it wasn't strawberry season, so strawberries were looking a little rough. I proceeded to watch my mom yell at the kid at the produce section (because it was his fault, right?) and then quickly proceed to ream the cashier and then finally the manger. The whole time, I slowly backed away from her and tried to plead with the people with my best puppy dog eyes that I was sorry. In short, my mom regularly lost her mind over some of the smallest things.

And it wasn't just over fruit, she did this with me too. As a kid, I was never sure what was going to set her off. One minute things would be totally cool, and the next minute Mrs. Hyde walked into the room where I proceeded to get cussed out for whatever happened to be on the menu for that particular day. While doing this, she often looked like a crazy person, and when I looked at her, I remember thinking I could not understand her at all. And her face…#momface

Then there were Sundays, oh holy bloody Sundays. It seemed like every Sunday before church there was a huge fight. I was not the only one on the other side of her anger- she was pissed at her husband too. I would get woken up abruptly by both of them yelling and mom running through the house, throwing shit, and screaming like a lunatic. Still, I just didn't know why.

It was always the small stuff. She did really well with the big stuff. I didn't make this connection until much later in life. When I think back, I remember getting suspended in high school twice in my junior year. I remember thinking, when she found out she was going to murder me. I mean, if the episode over the strawberries was any indicator, surely getting suspended was a death sentence. I was baffled as I sat and listened while she was totally logical and rational about the whole event. I was so confused! I did receive a punishment, but she was calm throughout the whole thing. Mom was always calm through the big stuff. And I got in trouble a lot.

That is the kind of woman I grew up with. So, today, when I talk to people about how she *was*, I reiterate she *was* a crazy lunatic. It's one thing to watch your kids grow up- but I got to watch my mother grow up, and truthfully, that's been the most amazing part.

Her growth has also allowed "US" to grow. Her growth has allowed me to grow as an individual, and she has taught me by doing it herself what it means to grow as a person. Her growth has allowed me to talk to her about my perceptions of what happened as a kid and has allowed me to process my resentments with her. And often my resentments are simply my kid brain, not understanding, but by talking about them as a grown adult that has done extensive healing, we have been able to clear and release a lot of guilt, shame, and resentment on both our sides.

CHAPTER 5

MY ADDICTION

I could go on and on about my growing up and all the things I struggled with, but I'm going to skip forward and get to why we are here. Addiction.

As I have said, there wasn't just one thing that made me turn to drugs. I know a lot of other people that have much worse stories than mine and went down completely different paths.

It's hard to say when my addiction really grabbed a hold of me. Was it when I started taking drugs? When I was addicted to suicidal thoughts? Was it when I figured out that playing the victim got me out of a lot of things?

I always blamed one thing or another on my behavior.

The trauma did it, it is all the trauma's fault

Those kids bullied me

I'm gay so I'm going to hell anyway

I could go on and on for the excuses I had. None of them were real. When I lied, I knew I was lying and made a conscious choice. When I stole, I knew it was wrong and I did it anyways. Every single time I picked a drug up, I was making a decision.

I don't spend a lot of time talking about the actual drug use anymore. Mostly because I have a life beyond my substance abuse.

But sometimes because I am so well adjusted, having created a normal and happy life for myself and achieved a lot of things since my addiction, there are times where people will look at me and minimize my previous addiction issues.

At one point in my life, I minimized my addiction issues and it almost cost me my life because I relapsed thinking I was ok. When I relapsed, the world of drug abuse got much bigger for me.

I started putting heroin and cocaine in needles and injecting these things into my arms, feet, shoulders, wherever I could. Things got so bad, I prayed that I would get arrested. I knew I wasn't going to stop until there was an intervening force. I started getting really scared for myself. I knew I was going to die. I could tell you all the horror stories and it would probably make a much longer and more dramatic book, but for your sake and my own, I would much rather focus on what made me want to change. s

That's why you are reading this, so you can start understanding what you need to do to help your loved one struggling through similar things

The biggest change occurred for me wasn't when I started to suddenly change. It was when my mother started changing. She started letting me fail. My whole life, we had this dynamic that worked like this: When things got bad enough, she would come and rescue me. When she changed this pattern, it helped me change.

CHAPTER 6

THE SHIFT

T he best thing my mother did for herself when I was in the depths of my addiction was getting help for herself. It started when she went to a leadership retreat for corporate training. During the retreat, the facilitator's dug into people's personal lives because whatever patterns show up in your personal life will also show up at work.

Whenever she started feeling like she needed to swoop in and come get me out of my situation, she had a support system that reminded her why that wasn't the best idea. They gently reminded her how that pattern was causing me to not be able to live my own life and suffer my own consequences.

Her biggest fear is that I would die. This fear is the driving force that causes most parents to get sucked down into their child's addiction, lose themselves, and cause more harm by trying to control the fate of their child.

I was recently watching *Kungfu Panda* and there was a quote in the movie that Oogway (the turtle) said that I think about often, "One often meets his destiny on the road he takes to avoid it."

The more you try to save your child without the necessary education, skills, and strategies, the deeper and closer to death they often find themselves. Parents unknowingly support their child by keeping them in addiction longer, and the longer a person is in addiction, the greater the chances are that they will die. I know this is hard to hear, and your desire to put this book down may be strong.

This is simply pointing out the necessity for education, skills, and strategies. You wouldn't try to do surgery on someone without going to school to be a surgeon, right? If you did, as much as you wanted to save the person's life you were doing surgery on, you may unintentionally do more harm.

Many times, parents' objections to getting help for themselves is "It's not my problem, why should I be the one to get help, they are the ones that need help. Help them not me." You are correct, they have a problem, and their problems are impacting your life.

Have you ever had a boss that made a decision that impacted your work through no agreement or conversation on your end? More than likely, yes. And more than likely, you didn't go back to your boss and tell him you were just going to keep doing things the same way. We have to adapt to the outside world around us and gain new skills to handle the difficult situations around us. We may not like it, we didn't sign up for it, but to move forward effectively, it's what we have to do.

It's what my mother did for herself. She didn't change and grow because she knew it was going to save my life. She did it for herself, so she manages herself through my actions and she learned along the way one very important truth: She was powerless over my life and the direction it was going. She was not powerless over hers.

My mother was able to break her patterns that held me back from being able to suffer my consequences. As a result of her support system and awareness, I was forced to start facing my consequences.

There was a defining moment for us on the last day I used. I was at the brink of death, and I knew I couldn't continue living the way I was. My body was shutting down. To put it in perspective, I am currently 5'6 165 lbs., and on my last day using, I was 107 lbs.

Part 2: My Last day Using

My mom was in town for business, and we had a dinner date set up, but I was too high to make it. The story I had told her about why I had to miss our dinner was that I had hit a dog on the way, that I jumped the curve swerving and wrecked my car.

So, her thinking that I was just in a wreck and had killed a dog, the next day she reached out again to make sure I was ok.

My mom knew something was wrong, my phone had been cut off. She came to find me at my apartment. I wasn't there either. She started getting really worried and since her name was on the lease, she went into the apartment.

It was a war zone of paraphernalia. Her suspicions were confirmed. She finally found where I was and asked me if I was using. The minute she asked me, I knew I had a choice. I could keep lying and continue down this road where death was imminent, or I could tell the truth and maybe get help.

I told the truth and was so relieved that it was all ending I didn't even care she was mad. She had a right to be mad.

There was one particular sentence she said to me that really made me understand that things were going to be different between us from now on. She told me she was going to help me one last time, but she also told me that she was going to learn to live without me. She said if I chose to do drugs, she was not going to allow me to be around her, in her house, or anywhere near the family.

She told me that if I had killed myself, she would learn to live without me. I never actually believed she could live without me before. I always knew she would be there to catch me when I fell. But when she said those words, I knew I was on my own. It wasn't just the words -it was the energy behind the words. I knew she meant it. She had never said anything like that to me before, and from that moment on, our whole dynamic shifted.

It took my mom three years of hard-core healing, inner self-awareness work, and working with facilitators to help her get the inner strength to say what she needed to say to me and mean it. When I got back into rehab, I was committed to my own healing. However, this did not stop me from testing her resolve along the way. She maintained her own resolve of what she was willing to do for me and what she wasn't, and I had to start living my life without her support for the very first time. She never turned her back on me, but she allowed me to be an adult and take care of myself.

My mom allowing me to fail allowed me to commit to my success. We have been able to repair a lot of the damage that has been caused by my addiction.

Today, I continue my road of healing. I make sure I maintain a healthy lifestyle with an ongoing commitment to abstain from drugs and alcohol. I have an amazing support network of family and friends.

Throughout my journey, I have helped hundreds of parents gain a better understanding of what they need to do with their own loved ones in addiction.

CHAPTER 7

YOUR OWN JOURNEY

For parents that are experiencing a loved one in addiction, I'm sure you feel like every time you open your mouth and try to help your child, it's like talking to a brick wall. You are likely feeling exhausted, isolated, scared, and perhaps ready to throw your hands up.

Every move you make seems to be the wrong one. Your work life may be suffering because even though you are physically present at work, mentally you are not. All your attention and focus are drained from worrying about your child, and your performance at work suffers.

My mother struggled at work. She sat in meetings trying to focus on her team, but the minute she walked out of the meetings her stomach was tied up in knots, her chest tightened and all she could think was, "What the fuck am I going to do about my daughter?"

She felt isolated and alone. She didn't want to tell people what was going on out of fear of judgment, opinions, and that funny way they might start looking at her. In her role, appearances are important.

Maybe the people you work with have started noticing a change in you and not for the better. They may even say, "Open up! Let people know what's going on." But when you do, you may experience judgement or being treated a bit differently than before. This pushes you deeper into isolation and confusion.

So now what?! You can't talk to anyone; you don't know what to do or where to go. When you try Google and going into forums online or researching what to do and how to fix your child, you are left feeling more confused than ever. While perusing the labyrinth of online research on the topic, you find that one person says this, another person says that, and they all contradict each other. People argue with one another, and you're left just wanting to pull your hair out.

You still don't know what to do. You see the stories; you see the struggle. Maybe you take comfort in simply feeling like you are not alone, but you still feel hopeless because there doesn't seem to be any answers or solutions.

Have you even slept? Does exhaustion leave you sitting in the car crying at stop lights and begging the higher powers that be to just tell you what to do to FIX YOUR CHILD?

There are times when it seems like things may be starting to get better. Like maybe there is hope after all. It could be for a day. It could even be for a week or two at a time. You might say to yourself, "Yes! I think they are finally turning it around."

And then you find out it's all been bullshit. They've been lying to you, or they start back with the same shit.

Have you reached the point where you're just ready to throw in the towel and cut them out of your life because you can't deal with that sinking feeling and the anger you feel towards your own child?

Close your eyes for just a second.

Think about all of those feelings and that pain that you're in right now.

I want you to ask yourself this:

Do you want to continue feeling the way that you do right now for the next five to ten years? What about for the rest of your life? Do you want to continue repeating this vicious cycle?

Or are you ready to break it?

PART 2
THE FOUR STAGES:

Parents go through four different stages of the addiction process. The hope is that you never get all the way to stage four. But if you are the parent at stage four, there is still hope.

CHAPTER 8

STAGE 1

I REALLY DON'T KNOW IF THERE IS A REAL PROBLEM YET.

Stage 1 is a critical stage to intervene early. If you have an adolescent still in high school or a young adult in college that you suspect or have even caught using any kind of drugs or drinking a little more than what is comfortable, this stage is for you.

No, we don't know yet if a serious addiction problem is imminent. This is a precious stage- the one where the parents get an opportunity to be proactive in their child's potential addiction and possibly even stop it before it gets more serious.

I say that because when a person first starts using drugs, there is no way to know how things are going to go. Many people use drugs recreationally and never get to the point of a serious addiction. They are just experimenting.

During Stage 1, we get to be proactive and hope we don't get to Stage 2. I know people who have used copious amounts of cocaine and heroin and have miraculously put that stuff down on their own and led normal lives. From my perspective as a recovering addict, I don't understand how they did it, but they did. It does happen.

At Stage 1, you may have no idea what to do or what it means for your child. If you've caught them drinking or smoking a little pot, it's too soon to tell if they will move on to more dangerous drugs.

After all, there is a good chance you may have even smoked some pot or experimented with certain substances, and maybe you came out ok. Maybe you didn't and had to deal with your own addiction issues. In either case, it seems almost like a normal experimentation process of adolescence and young adults.

I have been in recovery for well over a decade now. I have heard tens of thousands of other addicts' stories. We all have a similar pattern to what we were looking for in our childhood that made us gravitate to drug use.

There are some serious red flags to be mindful of during this stage. Here are some things you can start doing NOW that will help you in the future:

If you see your child in this stage, it's time to take action now. These next few moves you make are critical. Here are some questions to think about:

Have they had difficulty connecting to other people since early in their life?

Do they seem sad and depressed or struggle with anger?

Did they experience a traumatic experience as a young child and seem to have a problem coping with it?

Do they have brothers or sisters they often get compared too?

Are they an only child that seems shy and isolated?

Are they hanging out with kids that also drink or use drugs?

Drug addiction/alcoholism is not really about drugs or alcohol. It's about trying to find a way to cope with feelings.

It often starts when kids feel different. They are struggling to find their place in the world, they have all these emotions, and they don't know what to do or how to deal with them.

They might be searching for a connection, and they find something and someone that makes them feel important. They find a substance that makes them feel good- it makes them feel like they are part of and like they finally belong. It usually starts with the most easily accessible things to teenagers like marijuana and alcohol, but it could be anything.

We often say marijuana and alcohol are "gateway drugs," but they are only gateways because that's what is around. If there are pills like Xanax, Percocet, or other prescription pain medications around, that's what is used. When there are cans of whipped cream around, that's what is used.

It can be ANYTHING that will change the way your child feels.

It is ok that you don't know what to do in this situation. You aren't supposed to. The worst thing you can do for yourself is nothing at all.

If you are a parent that has just discovered pot in your child's room or notice that your alcohol is not lasting as long as it used to, or tastes watered down, or you notice you don't have as many leftover prescriptions as you remember having, you need to take action now.

Most parents tend to overreact or underreact. Either, "What the hell are you thinking?? Or, "It's probably not that big a deal." What's needed instead is a clear head and some leadership moves. This way you can properly assess what's happening and set the conditions for your child to effectively deal with whatever is driving their need to use drugs – even if it is recreational.

CHAPTER 9

STAGE 2

THERE IS A PROBLEM. NOW WHAT?

A s the parent of a child who has been struggling, you can finally admit to yourself that there is a problem. So, what do you do now? You do what most people today do- peruse Google or ask friends and family to find some solution.

After hundreds of Google searches, and many late nights in the harsh glare of the computer screen, fear and confusion sink in a bit deeper. Next comes the denial: "Well, my son/daughter isn't capable of those kinds of things. They would never do anything like that so there maybe there isn't as big of a problem as we thought there was."

Google is an ocean of confusion and contradictions. One person says this; another person says the exact opposite. By the end of your Googling you more confused and fearful than ever. You might be thinking:

So, am I supposed to kick them out or not?

Am I supposed to bail them out or not?

Do I really have to spend $20,000 to $60,000 to get them help? And even that still may not help?

What are all these different kinds of treatments? Is one really that much better than the other?

My kid has to go get on drugs to get off drugs; I don't understand?

This doctor says this is the treatment that works while that doctor over there says the exact opposite and that this is what works. Who is right??????????

It is impossible to find solid information about what to do with addiction on Google. Here's the thing about addiction: there just isn't a blanket solution. Unfortunately, what works for one addict may not work for another addict.

My own journey was very personal, and that worked for me. I've known thousands of addicts that get clean and stay clean. We each have our own personal stories of what worked for us. The outcome was the same, though our own journeys were very different. Your child is going to have to find their own way.

And it's important for you to find your own way building off your own foundation as a parent while using solid and effective strategies.

While they are finding their way, I see a lot of parents getting in their child's way, trying to control the outcome. This is a dangerous game because parents unknowingly support keeping their kid in addiction longer.

The longer someone is in their addiction, the higher the chances are of their child overdosing.

Many times, parents think that if their child just stops using drugs, then everything will be fine. We will send them to rehab and when they get out, all is fixed.

Stage 2 is really the budding of a much more serious addiction to come. In the early stages of addiction, the person using drugs and alcohol are in their own stages of denial. They probably don't really know they have a problem yet. And even if they do think they have a problem, they are probably minimizing the seriousness of it.

Her is the challenge for the parents: They are still thinking that if their child would simply stop using drugs, everything would be o. But here's the thing.

Drugs are merely a symptom of a much deeper issue.

Parents often use up all their energy, money, and time trying to focus on their child, while the child might want to stop using drugs because they recognize that is destroying their lives- but they don't want to work on the reasons they are using drugs to begin with.

Even the addict themselves think that if they stop using drugs for a period of time then they can go back to the less harmful substances and lead a normal life.

This is incorrect. Things are going to get a lot worse before they get better. They are going to progressively increase their crazy insane behavior. And they are going to drag you into it if you allow them to.

You are going to start acting in ways you never saw yourself acting and doing things to try to control their behavior that you never imagined yourself doing. You will say and do things you told yourself you'd never say or do. This is a family disease. It is also a progressive disease. The family members start progressively becoming immune to the chaos their loved ones are causing.

Sometimes parents get to the point where they start normalizing their own insane behaviors. Parents will:

Scoop pee out of a toilet to try and get a drug test to confirm their suspicions.

Follow their kids to the bad neighborhoods to see what is really going on.

Put tracking devices on their kids

Bail them out of jail constantly and let them continue to live with them to ensure their safety.

Turn a blind eye to everything they know is going on because they just can't face the truth or don't know how to handle it.

Start believing their unbelievable stories.

If you haven't gotten there yet, you will. If you don't get help for yourself to navigate this stage, we move into stage 3 of addiction.

CHAPTER 10

STAGE 3

SICK AND TIRED OF BEING SICK AND TIRED

Stage 3 of the addiction process is more than frustrating for the parents. At this point, you KNOW addiction. You are an expert having done the family therapies, putting your kid through rehab several times, watching them almost die over and over.

Things start to feel hopeless, like you won't ever see your child actually grow up and get the life you have always wished for them. You really start to KNOW it's only a matter of time before they die.

You are tired of the lies, the manipulation, and just the overall bullshit that you are ready to pack up and move out of town, so you don't have to see their face anymore.

So much hurt, anger, and resentment have set in that you have lost your own soul through the process and you don't think you will ever be happy again.

But there is still that small sliver of "I am not going to let my child die, they are my child, and I am still trying to find a way to help them."

This is the stage at which parents have lost trust in themselves. They don't know what to believe anymore, they don't have faith in themselves. Every time there seems to be just a little bit of hope they grab on to, their child reminds them they are full of shit and either relapse or were never actually clean in the first place. It was all a sham.

Relationships that parents have with other people in Stage 3 are getting closer and closer to nonexistent. They are growing weary of listening to other people's judgments. Especially all those unwelcome opinions of what *they* would or would not do if it *their* child were doing such things!

The isolation can be overwhelming. They don't want to tell other people what is really going on anymore, so they are left trying to save their child all on their own.

Here's the dangerous part of this stage: Death seems so imminent that parents go all in to trying to control the addict. And they know just enough about addiction from being around it for a period of time, they've educated themselves on everything thing there is to know about addiction, and they've read all the books. Basically, parents have earned an honorary PhD in addiction.

In short, they know just enough to really cause a lot of damage. This is the stage of survival at this point. The whole family gets stuck in this survival mentality, and there is not a clear line of communication. Clear and rational thoughts are not existent in survival mode.

The fear and anxiety are palpable. There is no time to think about anything else.

Work Life at This Stage

In terms of your work life, presentism is at its highest. You're at work, but are you really there mentally? Your performance has gone down. You may even be close to losing your job. No one at work knows what is really going on, all they see is someone that is not performing as well as they used to.

Maybe due to your position at work, you could never tell anyone.

Many of the clients I work with are senior executives and confidentiality is imperative for them. Because of the confidentiality they require, it's incredibly challenging to find someone that can help them.

The mindset with executives of corporations is you have a lot of really high level, incredibly intelligent people. They may be leaders of their organization, they know how to get shit done, how to go into an unfamiliar world and try to control it. What I see happen a lot is the parents are willing to pay exorbitant amount of money for someone else to come and "fix their kid," because that is what they are used to.

The mentality here is: The more money I spend on my kid, the better their chances are right?

NO. We have a society that has created this impression that if you want the best, you just pay more, and you will get you the results you want. If you want the best education for your kid, you pay for it. If you want the best car, you go out and buy it. The best house, the best whatever, etc....

The mentality I see most often with parents is, "that less expensive rehab didn't work so if I pay more for the high end one, then that will totally fix my kid." The next thing you know, you have spent thousands of dollars...AND THEY ARE STILL FREAKING USING. WHY?

Because money doesn't matter when it comes to addiction. YOU can't pay ANYONE to "FIX" them. It doesn't work. The addict has to decide when they are ready. Then, they have to become desperate enough to become willing to put in the work it takes to get clean and more importantly, stay clean.

You can't throw money at this problem and make it go away. I'm sorry. On the parent's side, this is the journey of YOUR personal work and self-discovery.

However, don't confuse this by thinking, "I shouldn't send my kid to rehab at all." That's not what I'm saying. My mom paid for both of my rehabs and it was not a waste. The first time, I learned a lot and got a lot of good information that I needed. When I relapsed, she paid for my second and final time. I was on my own after that, but I still had all that information in my head.

She made it very clear on the second go around it was her absolute and final time helping me and she would help only if I was truly ready. I was at that point, and I told her this. It would be hypocritical of me to say don't send your kid to rehab. But they should want to go and be ready to go if you are going to invest a lot of money.

Remember, there is a difference between spending money and investing money.

CHAPTER 11

STAGE 4

I'M DONE

This is the loss of the relationship with the child. You have been burned one too many times, the resentments and anger are too great to overcome. You have accepted that fact that they might die, and you will have to learn to live with that because it is hopeless to do anything about it.

You have done everything you could ever do, and they have broken you. They have taken everything from you, and you have nothing left to give at this stage.

Parents have lost their houses, lived in their own cars, lost their jobs and their careers over their kids' addiction. And they have received nothing but more pain and suffering because they spent all their money, time, and energy, and there was never a return on their investment. Their kids are still in the same place as they ever were, or even worse.

If you are here at this stage, I don't need to go on about what it looks like. You already know because you have graduated with

43

your metaphorical PhD program and you are done. You give up on your kid, they are hopeless.

What to do at each stage

Each one of these stages has its own set of challenges. You have to do different things depending on where you are at. A lot of parents think they are in one stage, when really, they are in another. This is what you do at each stage:

Stage 1: Get help for yourself

Stage 2: Get help for yourself

Stage 3: Get help for yourself

Stage 4: Get help for yourself

Did you just get a little upset because you thought I was going to tell you the answer?

I did! You thought there was some magical simple solution that would fix all your problems, right?

There is no overnight solution to this problem because the problems that created the addiction in the first place didn't happen overnight.

Many parents have hope that I am going to be able to give them their silver bullet. The one-sentence answer to all the problems of the world. I have not. I have, however, created a system that is the closest thing to a silver bullet you will find out there.

As I have said previously, each person is different. Addiction is a family disease and each family has their own way of understanding each other and doing things. What works for some may not work for others because it's not the system the addict grew up in. You have to find help for yourself so that the support and help are tailored specifically to your needs and the dynamics you have with your child.

CHAPTER 12

THEY MIGHT DIE

W hat we are facing right now in America are some very scary statistics we've never seen before in drug abuse.

I was just talking to a mother the other night, and she was telling me how she was recently talking to her daughter. She was saying how scary it is right now in the schools. The drugs that used to be in the schools versus the drugs that are in the schools right now are different. She noticed that it used to be that schools had certain cliques of people like the geeks, the nerds, the jocks, the loners, etc., that were smoking pot or something like that. These were the type of cliques that so many people were used to growing up with.

Her daughter commented on how they didn't have the kind of drugs that are in our schools now. Cocaine, Heroin, Meth, and that dreaded Fentanyl that seems to be causing the most overdoses. So, this epidemic is real and it's scary. The statistics are skyrocketing at alarming rates. Young people are dying.

I'm so grateful that I got clean when I did. Because it's a much scarier world now. The need is much more immediate. There have always been overdoses. But even in the last few years since I got clean (and I've been clean for over a decade now), that stuff has changed.

Even the people in the recovering community are talking about it because we lose so many people now. We just look at each other and are in so much pain and grief over the number of people and friends and family members that we're losing at an alarming rate.

Did you know that 200 people die a day from direct overdose? This does not include all the indirect causes of death due to drug and alcohol abuse. From 2016 to 2017, there was a 9.6% increase in overdose rates. This is an astonishing increase in one year, and it keeps rising.

Overdose has become the leading cause of death for people under 55.

This is so profound that it has caused the overall life expectancy to go down. Here is the good news- you don't have to be stuck anymore.

You don't have to cut your child out of your life or continue to live this way. You can break free of your child's addiction and allow them the freedom and desperation to start their own process of getting better.

I am going to tell you something might be hard to hear. The more you try to save your child from death, the more times you continue to swoop and rescue them because you think they will die if you don't, the higher chances they have of killing themselves.

How? Why? You are probably wondering how this can be true, and how it could possibly make sense. The first and very important lesson for is this: you cannot save them. They might die. And there is nothing you can do about that.

Are you shaking your head right now? Did you have a desire to throw this book across the room and yell that I am wrong and think that you still can save them?

You will lock them up if you have to, right? You will send them to jail, you will put them in a psychiatric hospital, you will quit your job to babysit them and make sure they are breathing during the night.

And you can do all of those things, and they still might die. And in the process, you lose everything yourself along with your child.

The more you go out of your way to save them, to lock them up, to rescue them, the more you are killing them. You are also creating a scenario for yourself where you will potentially finding them overdosed under your own roof.

I'm not talking about the normal concern parents have for their children. I'm talking about that paralyzing fear and desperation you are feeling about your child being in their addiction and the NEED to do something about it.

There are certain areas I'm going to really focus on where parents tend to make the most mistakes and need some extra help in. I've laid them out clearly for you below, so when you are dealing with your child, you can remember to pay close attention to the following five areas.

PART 3:
THE FIVE AREAS

These are the five areas where parents make common mistakes. At the end of the book, I am going to tell you my proven system that will help you see the changes you need.

Terminology Disclaimer: I use the word "mistake." I want to make a couple of things clear when using that word. I use that word in the broader sense that we as human beings make mistakes and we have lessons to learn in life. It is not to make anyone feel judged, guilty or take blame for anything, but simply to create an awareness on some areas that people tend to struggle with and can accidentally do things that are unintentionally contributing to an individual's substance abuse.

CHAPTER 13

AREA 1

DENIAL

This is a very difficult one because you don't know what you don't know.

There are a few different forms of denial parents experience when dealing with their loved one.

It's the people they are hanging with.

The most common form of denial is blaming other people for their child's behavior and drug use. You may be thinking it's the people they are hanging around with that are the trouble. If they would just stay away from them, they wouldn't be using drugs.

Maybe you've even tried moving your kid away to give them a fresh start, and you see the same things happening. That is because the other aren't the problem.

I moved around a lot in my addiction, always anxious to get a fresh start. When I went to college, I didn't even complete the first year, and moved home with my mom for a few months, still struggling to find myself.

One night, I didn't come home. I stayed over at someone's house because I was too drunk and high to go anywhere else.

I came home to my mom putting together a file of pictures and descriptions for the police just in case.

Things were clearly not getting better for me so we thought maybe a change of scenery would do me good. I went to Iowa to live with my dad for a few months.

I tried to go to school out there and get a couple of college classes under my belt, but I didn't go to class. I was a hot mess out there in Iowa too. I didn't really understand myself. I truly did not know why I kept just falling into the same patterns and finding the same types of people everywhere I went.

I came back to my mom's house for a while, then I moved in with this guy a few hours away. I knew that would do me some good- to get away from my parents and start really adulting.

And the SAME shit kept happening. Only this time, I got a job. I started working for a country club and the drugs there were better than ever. All I had to do was go to work and I was supplied with anything I wanted.

If I wanted cocaine, I'd go to the bartender. When I wanted oxycontin or Percocet, I'd go to the chef. When I wanted to smoke some crack, the head server was the guy to go to. And there just seemed to be an endless supply of pot wherever I went. HOW DID THIS KEEP HAPPENING?

To make a long story short and not stray too far from the point- no matter where I went, I took myself with me. The drugs were not really the problem, getting away and starting over wasn't the solution. Location and surroundings did not matter. Ultimately, I had to start fixing and healing the deeper roots of what was causing me to seek the drugs out in the first place.

To this day, I can go anywhere and as far removed as I am from the drug-using world, if I wanted to go find it, I'd have anything I wanted in 24 hours or less. So, it was never about where I was, or who I was hanging out with, it was always about me. My parents and family members were blaming my surroundings, and so was I.

Things continued on, and eventually, I got married to a guy that introduced me to a new darker world of drugs. The whole time, I remember thinking that if he would stop, I would be able to stop. He never stopped, and it wasn't until I was almost dead that I had the realization that it wasn't his fault. He did not do this to me, I was doing it to myself. I had a choice at any time to make a different decision. I did not.

They just need to stop using drugs

The other most common type of denial is parents think their kid isn't an addict at all. They accidentally got themselves addicted to drugs. Maybe you think if you lock them up in rehab whether they want to go or not, they will be fine once they get the drugs out of their system.

This form of thinking actually hinders the addict from getting any better. Mostly, because it gives them a way out. Parents even think that If they just get off the drugs for a minute, everything will be fine.

They go to rehab, get home, and *nothing changes because nothing changes.* They don't do anything to fix the problems that made them drink and use drugs in the first place. They just fall back into all their same patterns of behavior.

They did not accidentally get themselves hooked on drugs. It was a series of many choices they made based out of a need to hide from themselves, which is the underlying cause of their drug use.

Comparing your kid to others

When you go to Google or talk to other family members about their experiences going through their own child's addiction, some of the stories you hear may be later about the stages of addiction. You may not have gotten there yet, so you keep thinking maybe it's not an addiction, and your child is different.

You compare the worst of the worst stories and start minimizing how bad your child is. Maybe it's not really addiction because they haven't stolen from me…yet.

Or, they have stolen from me, but they aren't violent towards me yet. S(he) is a good kid, we raised them right, they will pull themselves out of this because they know right from wrong. They would never act like those other kids; they just aren't capable of that sort of thing.

Sometimes parents fall victim to actually listening and believing what their kids are telling them about themselves. Remember, the kid is in denial too, because their brain is being altered by substances. They might say things like:

There is no problem

I'm not as bad as this person

I can stop anytime I want

I'm not hurting anyone other than myself, why are you worried about it?

I'm an adult, I can do what I want

Your denial is not helping them.

We know when things are off. We may not always know specifically what it is, but we know when things are off.

For example, way back when in my early recovery days, I was married, and we used together. We also got clean together. We didn't stay clean together.

Around six months into our recovery, he decided to go and get high. He was lying and hiding it from me.

We got high together, so I know what he looks like when he is getting high. One night, he left the house at three o'clock in the morning. This is not normal behavior. He came back maybe an hour or two later.

I woke up and asked him what he was doing. He actually tried to tell me that he couldn't sleep so he left to go clean the car.

"What do you mean you're going to clean the car?" I asked. That doesn't sound right. But when I got into his car, the thing was just as messy as it ever was. And you may be laughing, but the truth is I was in so much denial and so unwilling to face the truth in that moment, I believed him even though I knew deep down he was lying.

I just had too many other things to worry about, I didn't want to worry about him. I didn't want to worry about what he was doing. I was carrying on with my life.

Here's the thing. When it comes to your kid, I'm sure you've had those moments. You've had those moments where you've ignored your intuition. You don't want to go into the fight you know you are going to have. You don't want to face the truth, and you're almost scared that, well, what if you're wrong?

What if you confront this and you're wrong, and then you have to deal with the fact that you didn't believe them? What if some of that comes into the guilt and shame area for you and your child, which you'll read more about later in this book.

This is why the first thing I work on with parents is: *remember to trust your instincts.* Yes, they are going to manipulate you, make you feel horrible for not trusting them, and tell you all kinds of things about your parenting that makes you want to not face the truth.

All the deceit and manipulation can make you forget to trust yourself.

Something else to remember, they have taught you how to treat them through the years of manipulation and lying. They have to be responsible that they have set those conditions up. So, no matter what, you can't feel guilty for not believing anything they say.

When I was early in my recovery, even though I wasn't using anymore, it didn't mean my mom trusted me. That took a long time and a lot of action on my part to show her I was a different person.

I couldn't even get upset when she didn't believe me. I honored her distrust in me because I had earned it! I didn't get mad. She helped me pay for my college education, but one of the conditions outlined in our deal was that before she gave me money, I had to pass a drug test. This was fair.

I had six or seven years clean and was doing really well, and I was still taking drug tests because that was the conditions we laid out in the beginning. She knew I was not getting high, but that didn't matter, we set guidelines out and we stuck with them till the end. And I never got upset, I never challenged it because I did not mind taking drug tests. It's easy to take drug tests when you know you're going to pass!

I have a lot of parents that start doubting themselves when their kids challenge their expectations and boundaries. Maybe their kid refuses a drug test. Does that mean they are getting high, or am I being a bad parent for not trusting them?

It means they are getting high.

Common excuses to try and get out of a drug test

- I just went to the bathroom a few minutes ago, I can't right now.

- I've been doing good, you should just trust me now

- I'm grown, I don't need to pee for you

If they are trying to get out of the drug test or delay it, you need to listen to your instincts. You have your answer; TRUST IT. Believe in yourself enough to know they have given you the answer you need.

And now it's time to defend those boundaries you have created.

If they pee for you and it comes out positive, but then they start trying to make you believe it was an accident, or they have excuses, DON'T BELIEVE THEM!!!!

Common excuses for failed drug tests

- It must be something I ate

- I took headache medicine

- I had a poppy seed muffin

- It must be the supplements I'm taking showing a false positive.

- It's a faulty drug test

- I was at a party and someone must have been smoking pot around me

- I smoked someone else's cigarette and it must have been laced with something. I swear I didn't know.

Nope, don't buy that bullshit. There are some over the counter drug medications that will cause false positive, here's the trick. Addicts that are taking drug tests KNOW how to get around them.

They know what to say and what over the counter medications will show up as a false positive on rare occasions. They will use that as an excuse so here is the red flag: They sit you down and google it to show you some website that says certain common over the counter medications cause false positives.

Certain websites even state Advil as one of them…GOOD GRIEF!! I've taken headache medicine before a drug test and it did not come back positive. That's just ridiculous.

They are prepared and ready for you to not believe them and have armored themselves with proof. Once again, you have to trust yourself, believe in your instincts, and act accordingly.

Here's where you will end up if you don't believe in yourself. Many parents have lurked behind their addicted children that are living with them after they go to the bathroom, waiting for them to forget to flush the toilet. They go in after the addict has used the bathroom and scooped pee out of the toilet to get a drug test.

It will confirm your suspicions yes. But if you have gone so low to normalize scooping pee out of the toilet after your child, you need to address a problem within yourself.

What I mean is, you have started becoming so immune to the insane behaviors, you have lost yourself in their chaos and you are simply desperate to do whatever it takes to help your loved one.

You are losing your confidence and your ability to trust yourself.

This is why I spend so much time helping parents. Learning to trust yourself again can take a long time.

I'm really too busy to deal with this right now

Many parents I work with have high-level careers that keep them very busy and consumed with their own work. Finding out your child is using drugs simply doesn't fit into your schedule. You don't have the mental bandwidth to think about that right now.

There is no shame in wanting your child to act like an adult and feel as though you should be able to focus on your career and not have to worry about them. You ARE too busy to deal with their chaos. However, the decisions being made while ignoring the facts can sometimes unintentionally support their drug habit.

What ends up happening is the problems get ignored. Then the loved one continues to progress in their addiction until a major event happens and you are forced to face the truth. By the time you are facing the truth of what's really been going on, it becomes a lot more reactive.

Many times, parents simply don't know what to say and how to handle the situation. They don't know what questions to ask, how to manage their emotions through being lied to or stolen from.

Parents feel a sense of betrayal when their own kid lies to them or steals from them and instead of handling the core issue of what is going on with their loved one. They get angry and resentful and have a tendency to lash out.

CHAPTER 14

AREA 2

FINANCIAL

The second area parents struggle in is knowing how to handle financial The second area parents struggle in is knowing how to handle consequences and expectations.

Some of these include things that you may not have considered, particularly in terms of how to protect yourself. I'll give you an example. My mom wrote me out of the will in the midst of my addiction. And it was the best thing she could've ever done because she did not want something to happen to her and leave me with access to money.

I was going to kill myself. If I had received a large sum of money, there's no doubt in my mind that I would have killed myself with it. Not intentionally. But yes, I would have definitely gotten enough drugs to overdose, because even without money I was close.

You don't want to give someone doing cocaine and heroin money. They'll die. Fast. So, she started protecting me financially in a lot of ways, and it took her a while to know and understand that she had to do that.

It was really difficult, because at some point, she actually had to ask the family to stop giving me money. It was a tough and smart decision. We had to do things differently.

There's a lot of other things out there that you probably don't even think about. I help parents with understanding the right moves to make financially with their own kids. My situation is different than your situation so what worked for me may not work for you.

There are so many other ways to harm your kid financially other than just giving them money directly. Money is needed to buy drugs, but money is also needed to pay rent, bills, food, etc.

Many times, parents are helping pay for the necessities, even though their loved one is working and SHOULD be able to pay for their own bills, but they don't. The kid is spending their money on drugs, and the parents are paying for everything else. You are indirectly supporting their drug habit.

There are so many times I have fallen for the sob stories of addicted friends. And these are just my friends. It is a million times harder when it's your own child.

These friends give me a sob story about how bad their life is, and they can't even afford a jar of peanut butter or gas to go to the grocery store to get food. So, I've taken them to the gas station and buy them gas, trying not to unintentionally support their habit, but loving and supporting them as a good friend would. We know better than to just give them money, right?

And then, later on, that evening, they had enough gas to go drive over to the drug dealers house, which was their ultimate goal. Not the grocery store, not taking their mom to the doctor, but the damn drug dealers house. And I participated in them getting high. I don't feel shame because the lying and manipulation belongs to them, but it was a little bit of a wake-up call for me to be more diligent.

Financial boundaries are tough. Parents often think it just comes to not giving them money. But if you are letting them live with you, that means they don't have to pay rent. So, any money they make that doesn't go to rent goes directly to drugs.

Maybe they don't work at all. Why do they need to work if you are giving them a place to stay and buying their food for them? They get to hang out all day with their friends and find people that will get them high.

Parents challenge me on this area constantly, "Well, I am not going to kick them out and make them live on the streets." But here's the thing: if you set up rules and expectations for them and they break them knowing they are choosing to not have a roof over their head anymore if they don't follow your rules, then they are making a CHOICE.

They want to live on the streets. Allowing them to live with the choices they are making is the most loving and caring thing you can do for them. That's not tough love, that's just love, but it's tough to do. They are telling you what they want. YOU are not kicking them out, THEY are choosing to leave.

Imagine this, you give your loved one a car so they can get around. Maybe they need a car so they can get to work. Maybe you don't even pay for their gas- they have to work for that. But their addiction is so bad, they sell the car. They get a few thousand dollars for it.

That is enough to easily buy them enough drugs to kill themselves.

What about the tools in your garage? Tools can easily be pawned and often are. Have you ever gone into a pawn shop and half the pawn shop is tools and jewelry?

Or that nice digital camera you bought them for Christmas? (This was an item I pawned) Or their video games you keep buying them in hopes they get more addicted to their video games than to drugs?

Are you buying them gift cards instead of giving them money thinking you are outsmarting them? You're not if you just gave them a $500 gift card, they are going to sell it and get about $250 on the streets for it. That's enough for a nice little evening at home shooting enough heroin they could overdose with.

There are so many other subtle nuances to the financial area. That's why it's really hard to know and understand how you are actually participating in their substance abuse. Having someone really be able see and show you the subtleties and then what to do about it is the difference between participating in their death versus participating in their rescue. I know these nuances in and out, I can be your eyes.

I remind people there is a difference in investing in your child's future and simply spending money on them that does not support your intended goal.

I know there are some people that just read this section, and maybe are either a little offended or upset. Maybe it hit a little too close to home, and my only intention of pointing some of these things out is out of the safety for your child and for yourself. Pointing some of these things out is meant to help parents understand some of the rule's addiction plays under. Now, you can operate with more facts and make decisions with more information.

CHAPTER 15

AREA 3

GOOD PARENT SYNDROME

T he good parent syndrome aka "the rescue mentality." Swooping in at the last minute before they really get to suffer the full weight of their consequences isn't helpful.

Bailing them out of jail for the second, third, fourth time is not helpful. Giving them a nice warm bed because they got kicked out of their apartment or lost their house only tells them they can do whatever they want because you are going to bail them out and not make them suffer too much. They learn that they always have something to fall back on.

Your child does not have confidence in themselves right now. They feel like a failure and like they can't do anything right. I tell so many parents that their child is looking for love, looking for connection. It's the same kind of thing a child does from a young age when they act poorly to get their parents attention.

As a person who has experienced this, I did feel like a black sheep of the family. Like I was the ultimate screw up. I knew my mom loved me, that was never the question.

Subconsciously, I liked it when she would come in and take care of my problems.

I knew if my mom had my back, I would be ok. No matter what was happening to me in my life, my safety net was there. I could screw my life up, and my mom would come in and help me fix it. In a weird and very unhealthy way, this was the way I was seeking her approval. I didn't know any other way at the time. And it was working, so I used it for as long as I could.

There were numerous times she helped me move so I could get a fresh start. There were times she would protect me by pulling out her mama bear on people who were upset with me and putting them in their place. She would look at people and tell them how things were going to go with me and exactly what they were going to do to help me.

I never went to jail, even though I deserved to. But I knew if I DID go to jail, she would have helped me out, at least before she started setting her own boundaries toward the end of my using.

Prior to that, just at the brink of failure, she would swoop in and save me from completely falling on my ass. It was awesome, or so I thought.

I didn't understand at the time that her doing this made it difficult for me to actually grow up. I didn't have to be fully responsible for my actions, and as long as I didn't have to take full responsibility, my addiction was able to progress because, "Fuck it. It's not my problem or my fault."

The truth is, if she hadn't started making those changes in herself and the way she handled me and started allowing me to feel my consequences, I may have never grown up. I would still be fighting my addiction today IF I happened to still be alive.

I see where I am today. 12 years later. I know how much work I had to put into getting to where I am today, but I would have never been willing to do that work as long as I had someone around to always catch me when I fell.

The first time I tried to get clean, I stayed clean for two years before I relapsed again. I did all the obligatory things during that time. I worked on myself, did the meeting thing, had the network, friends, etc. I was technically the poster child of recovery. I fed people what they wanted to hear.

There is this thing in recovery we call "Cash Register Honesty." It means we stop stealing, lying to other people, and maintain that basic level of honesty. You can trust us to not rob you or steal from you, or even lie to you. And cash register honesty is great but what I was missing was the honesty with myself.

Addiction is messy, recovery is messy. Life doesn't all the sudden just get better because I quit using drugs. I had to start facing some shit. I had to start dealing with my consequences and I didn't even have the drugs anymore to cope with the feelings of those consequences. I was a hot mess, but I was taking responsibility for the first time in my life.

This was not pretty. When I was really honest with myself and others, I was in so much pain there were times I just couldn't breathe. My mom did not trust me. I would test her commitment to the boundaries she set. I tested her willingness to allow me to be on my own and deal with my own problems.

When I left my husband, I had over a year clean. I was trying to make ends meet on my own and grow up, be an adult, and fully support myself. Even though I was clean, I wasn't great with money.

I didn't know how to save money, how to plan for possible future incidents like my car breaking down or a surprise bill that came in the mail that I wasn't expecting. Sometimes, I simply got carried away with shopping too much (I still do if I am honest). Even with a year clean, a couple of times I went to ask my mom to help me pay a bill or two. She would pause and then tell me no.

It wasn't to be mean; it wasn't because she thought I was using. She just started treating me like an adult. She knew how much money I made, and that I should have been able to save money for surprise bills or be able to reign myself in from eating out and shopping too much.

She started treating me like an adult, and adults have to know how to deal with money. What that meant for me, is I had to grow up.

Later on, she decided she would help me with school. But we had conditions. I had a budget I had to work with, if I wanted things outside that budget, I had to get a job while going to school and work for the extra money. And most importantly, I had to show up for myself the whole time. I had to keep making the agreed-upon grades and doing the right things.

Sometimes parents know and understand their child may have suffered through a difficult childhood for whatever the situation was. This falls into the guilt and shame area, which we'll touch on shortly.

Parents will often partially understand why their kid turned out the way they did. Sometimes parents even blame themselves for it. I'll go more in details of how people use this to pull your hear strings in the guilt and shame section.

The next area is one of the biggest things we as a society talk about parents doing with their addicted loved one. It is also one of the more painful and mishandled areas. Boundaries.

CHAPTER 16

AREA 4

BOUNDARIES

I know that you're really good at setting boundaries. I know that you've said over and over, "This is the last time" or "I'm not doing this anymore," or "If you do this again, I'm kicking you out of the house" or "I'm not paying your rent anymore and I'm not bailing you out of jail."

Some of those boundaries you upheld and maybe some of them you didn't.

Sometimes It can be important to understand why we are setting the boundaries to begin with. What is this boundary going to do for your loved one? How is it going to help them?

Maybe all you see your boundaries doing is hurting them because it may involve putting them out on the street and letting them deal with some severe consequences, like leaving them in jail. All you're seeing is the pain that you're causing your kid and not understanding how valuable it is for your kid to experience that.

This is an important and vital mindset shift and it's about believing in your boundaries. When you believe in your boundaries, it also means that you have to believe in yourself. s

HOW to set boundaries and WHEN to set them is crucial to maintaining firm boundaries. Here are a few tips to remember when you set boundaries.

Don't set boundaries from a place of emotion. If you set emotional boundaries like your kid does something and you get mad and start telling them, "Shit's going to change dammit!" Let's say you set all your boundaries from that emotional state. When those emotions dissipate, many times the boundaries disappear as well.

You may kick them out in the heat of the moment and maintain that state of firmness and anger for a period of time. But eventually, that anger will start to wane. And they will start making you feel sorry for them again.

And then you let them back into your house because you feel bad and like a bad parent for getting angry and kicking them out. You start doubting yourself like maybe you overreacted out of anger, and the vicious cycle continues.

A second tip I tell parents when setting a boundary is that it can't be about you trying to control their behavior. That's just setting you up for failure and they aren't going to just stop doing what they are doing because you tell them to.

It should be in more of the form of "If you do this...then this is what will happen." Here's the trick, you have to actually DO the thing you said you would do. They are absolutely going to call your bluff if you don't, and the cycle continues.

The third tip: If you are simply making up boundaries with no intentions on keeping them, those aren't good boundaries. You have to believe in the boundaries you are setting so when it comes time to upholding them, you will.

Remember, if you tell them the consequences and they CHOOSE to break your rules, they are the ones choosing what they want their life to look like. Let them live with their choices.

Boundaries are very personal. There is no one that knows your child better than you. What works for some people in their situation may not work for you. You may not be ready to set certain boundaries. You may not understand why you have to set certain boundaries.

My experience in working with different parents in many different ways, tells me that every parent has a different way of doing things. It's important to find your own way through this process and set boundaries you feel you believe in for your child. But it is also imperative that you have someone in your life that can help you define boundaries that are effective.

I work with a lot of addicts. I help a lot of addicts, providing them the tools and resources they need to help themselves get clean and stay clean. But not everyone in my life gets clean, actually, the majority don't.

I've had to really work on my own boundaries. And I've had to be very clear with what my boundaries look like.

Sometimes situations happen, and I fall victim to their manipulation and move the line of my own boundary. It happens. I try not to beat myself up for it anymore because when they lie and manipulate, it's not about me. It's not them doing anything TO me. It's about what they are doing to themselves and being very good at getting what they want.

I have to remain diligent in understanding where people can find their way in to use me. Often, this comes from my own doubts and insecurities about myself.

They call me a bad friend and say I should be there for them no matter what. Ouch, that hurts, maybe they are right.

They will say things like, "Do you really want me to die, I need this right now." NO, I DON'T WANT YOU TO DIE, I'LL SAVE YOU! I wouldn't be able to live with myself if they died. It would be all my fault if "I turned my back on them."

This lie goes back to the "You Can't Save Them" chapter. Go have a second look if you need to be reminded that it is NOT YOUR FAULT. I knew as long as my goal was to save their life, they were going to manipulate me into doing whatever they wanted.

That fear is so powerful and so strong until I embraced that they actually could die and that it wouldn't be my fault and there was nothing I could do about it, I continued to fall victim to their manipulations. I had to face a level of powerlessness I would not wish on anyone, but here we are. I was going to have to start thinking about my life without them.

I also know that if I allow those doubts and insecurities about the potential for blaming myself for another person's death, I would continue to support their addiction and contributing to their potential overdose.

I've told friends that use the dying tactic on me that I would be very sad, and I would go to their funeral and grieve their death, but I was not going to buy them drugs. And when I said it, I had to mean it, because I didn't actually know if they would live or not.

But this is your CHILD. I know that is what you are saying to yourself. That it's different and it doesn't apply here because we are talking about your child and not a friend.

The fifth area is the most complicated and THE most valuable area for parents to focus their attention on. Their own guilt and shame.

CHAPTER 17

AREA 5

GUILT AND SHAME

This is going to be the longest section I address, mainly because it's the most complicated and the biggest theme that ties all the other sections together. It's the theme that runs the deepest through both the addicts and the people around them that unintentionally and unknowingly support their drug and alcohol addiction.

Just a heads up, this is not going to be an easy section to read. There are going to be things said that you won't like to hear. My promise to you is the truth and to be real with you so you can save your child.

Family, friends, teachers, preachers, and society, in general, all play a major part in the formation of a person's addiction.

That being said, no one is to blame for the person's addiction other than themselves. The destruction of addiction is a series of conscious choices made. Every decision I made was my own. No one made me do anything.

Did I manipulate people around me to get what I wanted? Yes. Most of the manipulation was subtle and not always conscious. It was from years of being groomed and taught how to pull a person's heartstrings to let me off the hook.

To this day, if I so desired to spin the tables on people and make them feel bad so they don't get mad at me, I know how to do that. I know how to seek out a person's insecurities and use those just to manipulate them and justify my behavior.

It wasn't until I started taking responsibility for myself, for my actions, and for my life that I became the person I always knew I could be. Part of recovering from addiction is taking responsibility for yourself. But I didn't get there alone. People had to start allowing me to be held accountable for my behavior.

Victimhood is the cornerstone of a person's addiction.

Whatever trauma a person has suffered, they are still responsible for taking care of their emotional well-being in a healthy way. Letting people off the hook for their actions feeds into a person's victimhood.

My trauma did NOT make me steal from my mom. I stole from my mom because I needed money to buy things. I was stealing money from my mom long before drugs. I would steal money to buy candy. Why? Because I liked candy and I wanted it. Not because of my trauma but when I acted out in certain ways, I would throw my trauma up because I didn't want people to be mad at me. I would rather them feel sorry for me. And it worked. So, I kept doing it.

I have fallen victim to my own guilt and shame when addicts have been able to pull on my own heartstrings. I've had to do an immense amount of work on myself to handle myself with another addict.

I'll give you an example, I'll go back to my ex-husband again. Let's revisit the moment when I was in so much denial, back to that situation where I'm confronting him about getting high, while I kind of know deep down that's exactly what he's doing.

I even tried to bluff and tell him I was going to go get him a drug test. He was so good. He said, "you know what? You can give me the drug test, I'll pass it. But then we got to talk about our relationship, and how you don't trust me."

Ooh, now that hurts. Even though I knew he was getting high, he was able to manipulate me. He used that, "Oh, you don't trust me? Well, that's okay. I guess I'll just have to really think about that."

He did a really good job of using my own insecurities about our relationship to make me doubt myself, and that's just one example of many of the ways that guilt and shame can be manipulated.

When a parent or family member allows the guilt and shame to remain, it is easier for the addict to manipulate them into believing them, and into getting what they want.

For you, it may be your insecurities. They may be trying to blame you for their addiction. They may have even said this out loud. Maybe they've hinted at it. And as long as that guilt and shame are there, the addict will use it. But when it's not there and they don't have that leverage anymore and they can't use it, they actually have to start thinking about things differently.

They actually have to start figuring something else out. It will help them reach their point of desperation faster because they're not getting what they want and they're not able to use what they've always used before.

An addict's manipulation tactics:

Now that we are in the guilt and shame section, it's important for you to be aware of how addicts use manipulation tactics to pull on your heartstrings.

We grow up knowing what we can get away with when it comes to our parents. We know how to get their attention. and whether it's good attention or bad attention is really irrelevant. Attention is attention.

Subconsciously, we build belief systems from a young age, most of the time focusing on how we get our connection with others. How do we know we are loved? How do we know we are taken care of?

Through a lifetime of creating certain belief systems, we learn how to get what we need which is connection and love, a sense of belonging.

I grew up as an only child, and I was a pretty shy child. My mom was busy working to give me the best life possible. We joke today calling it, "winning the lucky embryo lottery." I am spoiled, it would be doing my mom a disservice to call my life anything less that great.

Growing up, I was left to my own devices a lot and being shy did not gain me many friends. Not only was I shy, I was a fairly angry and aggressive kid. I usually only ever had one or two friends at most, and they would get sick of me after a while.

We moved a bit in my developing years, so it was hard to really learn to connect with people. When I got into High School, my mom promised me she wouldn't move me again, but I lacked knowledge about how to be a friend.

I did start gaining some close friendships in high school but where I felt like I really belonged was in the secret clubs.

It started with the secret clubs of sneaking cigarettes. Even if the other people who were doing the same thing weren't really a friend, we had a mutual secret understanding.

Then there was a secret club of smoking pot, I would get to smoke pot with people that in the hallways, we didn't really speak much or hang out except in times where we did sneak off together and toke up. It was great.

I'd come back to class with this sense of belonging AND stoned out of my mind. Everyone sounded like the teacher from Charlie Brown. There was this shared bond I formed with people through that.

When I smoked pot, I wasn't angry and aggressive anymore. I wasn't much of anything other than a giggling eating machine.

I was simply a more pleasant person to be around when I was smoking pot. I didn't drink too much in high school but there were a couple of times I drank before basketball practice. I wasn't drunk, but just tipsy enough to have the best basketball practices I'd ever had.

When I drank some, I felt like I was the basketball player I always wanted to be. Fearless, willing to take risks, and I had the skills to back it up. I was fun and pleasant when I was tipsy. I wasn't the shy awkward kid.

You can see where this is going. But at the time, I had no idea what was in store for me.

All the same, reasons I started using drugs applied throughout my whole addiction. Needing to feel loved, a sense of belonging, and this secret club of connection and understanding. No one understands an addict better than another addict. I had found my people. The truth is, I didn't even like the drugs all that much. But they did help me cover up a lot of pain.

And as the pain grew because of all the bad things going on around me in my using, my using grew to cover up all the bad. It was a vicious, hopeless cycle of shame.

And I used my shame and I used my victimhood to get what I wanted.

I knew no matter how bad things got; my mom was always there to rescue me. When things got bad enough in one town, she moved me to another, and then another. She bailed me out of so many things and helped me "clean my life up" that I knew she would always get me out.

While my addiction grew, I didn't really know what to do when I lost my job, almost lost my place to live, and was about to die; but I knew the people around me weren't going to let me completely fail. They would always be there.

I did not know how deep my own mother's guilt and shame went with me and feelings like she was never doing enough or feeling like a bad mother. But even though I didn't fully understand her story and why she had so much guilt and shame, but I sure did know how to use it.

My favorite moments were when all hell broke loose around me through various points of my life was when my mother came in to save me. That's when I knew my mom loved me. That's the dynamic we had created. Subconsciously, I was taught that in order to get my mom's love, I needed her to rescue me. Sound familiar? Yep, she fell into her own "good parent syndrome."

I could go on and on about how much I used my own mother's guilt and shame and give you hundreds of examples.

But here is the bottom line for you. If you have any doubts or insecurities about your own parenting. If you have any guilt for the things you think you did to them as a child, they know it and are subtly using it against you.

If you are afraid that they are going to die, they are using that against you. If they start threatening suicide or hinting in any way they want to harm themselves, and you give in to what they want out of that fear, it is teaching them that they can use that against you.

If someone is threatening to harm themselves or kill themselves, you should hold them to their words and have them involuntarily committed. They obviously need help and they are asking for it by telling you they want to harm themselves.

Will they get mad at you? Yes! Will they try to hold that over your head? YES. But remind them that they asked you to do that by insinuating they were going to harm themselves. Legally you had no other choice. You chose to believe them.

You have to teach them how to treat you. If they start threatening you, treat them how they are asked to be treated, what would you do if a stranger came up to you and threatened you?

If a stranger broke into your house and stole from you, what would you do? If you did nothing at all when a stranger stole from you, they may come back and do it again because they know you wouldn't do anything about it. That is what you taught them.

If a stranger did something worthy of getting arrested for and they were thrown in jail, and they called you up and asked you to bail them out, would you? No, most likely you wouldn't. And if you did, they would probably just leave and go do something again to get them put back in jail because they know you are going to help bail them out.

You are teaching them you are going to bail them out of their problems.

If they spend all their money on drugs and don't pay rent and lose their place to live, they said by their actions that they want to be homeless.

My in-laws kept bailing me and my husband out of our rent troubles. We used all our money on drugs, couldn't pay rent, gave them some sob story and they would write us a check. It kept us in our addiction months longer. And in that time period, we both almost died several times.

By them bailing us out, it almost cost us our lives.

These five areas, I am sure some of this was hard. You may be on the edge of your seat waiting for me to say something about enabling or being co-dependent so you could throw the book down.

Having worked with and done extensive research, I came to an understanding of what parents are doing…The best they can with the information they are provided with. They are doing the best they can by loving and supporting their children the best way they know-how. Parents only want what is best for their child, and they will do anything to protect them.

These areas are meant to provide more information and more understanding of the illogical, chaotic, and destructive rules that addiction plays under so parents can operate with more information. More information and understanding about addiction means parents can do what they want to do, which is to protect their children.

CHAPTER 18

UNDERSTANDING AN ADDICT: WHY THEY CHOOSE DRUGS OVER EVERYTHING ELSE

I often get asked, "Why does an addict choose drugs over everything else? Their kids? Their family? Anything? Everything?

This is a million-dollar question that I am going to explain but you still may not be able to understand, unless you are an addict.

I don't know that anyone has THE answer to this question. Addicts don't even seem to have a satisfactory answer.

I can't explain to someone that has never experienced what it is like to knowingly choose the drugs over everything else. It's like trying to define the word "love."

Most of us at some point have experienced the emotion of love in some way. When someone says love, we can all connect to what that emotion feels like for us. It's the same for all emotions we feel like fear, anger, happiness, sadness, etc. When someone says these emotions, we connect to the emotion so we can understand them. But we can't quite define it very well in words.

If someone has never felt an emotion, there is no ability to connect and understand. Therefore, it can be difficult for someone who has never felt the drive to get drugs by any means necessary to understand what that emotion feels like. And any person that has felt this will tell you it is a very strong emotion.

Why do addicts do things they know are bad for them and everyone around them? There are so many things in my life I would like to be doing that would be good for me. I would love to meditate every day, do yoga, exercise, eat right, so many things! I don't do these things even though I know it would be good for me. I even have a DESIRE to do these things.

But my desire for cake trumps my desire to eat right. That is until I have eaten so much cake that I become fatigued all the time, I gain weight, which makes me depressed, and eventually, I start feeling suicidal. This is all over a damn piece of cake.

So, what do I do? I stop eating cake for a while, cut back on all sugary substances, and start feeling better. When I start feeling better, I get excited because my life feels normal again. Hurray!!! Problem solved...I shall reward myself with more cake. And the cycle continues.

The principles behind this cycle of eating cake are the same principles of what it's like for an addict, only it's a lot more dramatic and the consequences are a lot more immediate and severe.

When the consequences for the addict start showing up, it's easier to deal with those consequences when their drug of choice is involved. The deeper they go into their addiction, the more they want to escape from the destruction they are causing themselves. And the less they want to face what they are doing and the person they have become.

People use drugs because it feels good. It certainly feels better than facing their life. If I could use drugs without all those pesky consequences, I would in a heartbeat. Sounds crazy, right?

I do believe people deserve their consequences. I do not want to make out like I am making an excuse for us addicts who has made poor decisions. We deserve our families being mad and frustrated at us for our poor decisions. Hell, I was mad and frustrated with myself for years.

If we did something bad enough to land us in jail, we deserve to stay there. We deserved our spouse leaving us, our kids being taken from us, whatever the consequences were, we deserved them. Until we accept our personal responsibilities, we can't grow our inner strength and be the person we really are.

When trust is broken, we have to face the fact that we have to earn it back, if we ever can.

Desperation is what brings us to our knees and start wanting to make a different decision. Desperation will make us want to do whatever it takes to stop using. Until we are desperate enough, we won't stop. I became desperate enough when I knew I was going to die.

Actually, not even dying made me want to stop. Dying was going to be a relief. It was facing the fact that I might not die, and I had to continue living in the hell I was in. At that point, I became willing to face all my consequences. I didn't care anymore how mad everyone was at me, I was desperate to stop the insanity.

I stopped the insanity and started facing myself and my pain. Over a decade later, I continue to face my pain…and sometimes it sucks. There are some days I don't want to do anything anymore. But I don't use because I know I can't handle adding any more pain. I just have to deal with it and move on. FUCK!

I say all that to remind people that just because a person doesn't understand and can't comprehend what it is like for an addict that is using drugs, you can have compassion without judgment. You can set and DEFEND your boundaries with no guilt. As an addict, we are responsible for the decisions we make. In the depths of my addiction, I made choices. Choices that I knew were not ok. I just simply didn't care and did them anyway. I was never a victim to the disease. I did, however, victimize myself. I CHOSE to do drugs over my willingness to get help.

I know a lot of addicts are out there shaking their heads right now disagreeing with me about using drugs being a choice because many of us feel like it's not a choice when we are in the middle of it.

But the reality is, it is a choice. When I lied, I knew I lied. When I stole, I chose to steal. When I used, I was a willing participant. I could have made a different decision, and I didn't. This is accepting personal responsibility part of the game. And it sucks, it's painful, and seems impossible when we are in the grips of our addiction. Until things get bad enough for us, the choice to use drugs is the easier choice.

Hopelessness drives an addict to continue their drug use. People using drugs to the extremes start going into this hole of despair where they genuinely feel like maybe everyone is better off without them being around.

So, when an addict seemingly chooses drugs over their children, as illogical to a sane person as that looks, the addict feels like their kids are better off without them. They are safer with someone else. AND IT'S TRUE. s

It doesn't make them love their kids any less, but they know they can't quit, and they know they are a danger. They are actually choosing to protect their kids from themselves by letting someone else take care of them.

CHAPTER 19

WHAT DO I DO NOW?

One of the frustrating things I have encountered in all my research the lack of resources available for parents that have kids suffering from addiction.

A couple of dozen books have been written. Some of them are really good and inspiring. But inspiration only goes so far in actually changing a person's behavior and patterns.

Many times, I am talking to a parent that is incredibly frustrated with their situation and begs me to, "Just tell them what the solution is." "Jen, what's the answer here?" I wish I could wave a magic wand and just give an easy solution. I can't. But I can give you my direct experience, because I've been through it. The simple solution is change, and you need to change as much as the addict needs to change.

Remember, the problems that created the addiction didn't happen overnight, so the change isn't going to happen overnight.

In terms of my own recovery, I have had to find my own ways of doing things. What works for me may not work for everyone. I keep the core foundations of my recovery and what people suggest. But everything else is up for my personalized journey of self-discovery and transformation.

I've tried so many different things, and not everything was for me. For some, they have found that picking up running, going to the gym, or doing that crazy cross-fit stuff really works for them. I hate all that stuff, but people continue to suggest it for me, and I continue to ignore it because I've tried it and it's just not my thing.

Others have gotten really involved in yoga, traveling, and hundreds of other things, but again, I had to find my own journey.

A parent's journey is very similar. It's personal. You have your own denial that you are facing. And when you read and google search and find some of those denials that other people talk about, you can see them in yourself. But there is a host of other things you can't see, because you are simply too close to it.

Setting boundaries and defending them is very personal. You simply just may not be ready to set certain boundaries that people suggest. Maybe the boundary, such as kicking them out, you kind of know you probably should but you just can't do it. You're not ready. Maybe you can't bring yourself to leave them and jail and you keep bailing them out. Or you are paying their rent, or countless other things you know you probably shouldn't be doing but you just aren't ready to stop.

Your own journey through this process is imperative to the success of yourself and your loved one in addiction. You don't have to be willing to change everything overnight. Just have the willingness to start somewhere.

Addiction can tear families apart. The anger and resentments can cause the relationships between parent and child to become estranged. The healing process for the parent makes it so that when the addict starts changing, the relationship can also be repaired.

My relationship with my Mom could have easily become damaged so much so that we wouldn't have been able to repair it. But today, because of her willingness to change and grow along side of me, we have a great relationship.

One thing that has frustrated me about the support for parents, there isn't much out there. Group therapies are great, but they aren't for everyone. Sometimes parents just aren't ready to open themselves up to several strangers. Maybe they would be willing, but their job title prevents them from risking anyone finding out what is going on in their lives.

Can you imagine being the CEO of a large corporation or a politician and going through something like this? A position where you have to keep your private life private and someone suggests a group therapy? That's going to get a big hell no.

Our society has focused on forming a lot of different therapy models for the addict but not a lot of different resources for the parents. And certainly not many for the long-term support.

A few years ago, I had quite a few parents in these situations come to me asking for help. I would try to send them to resources, but it just wasn't helping them. I had a parent go to Al-Anon for six months and feel like they hadn't gotten anywhere.

I took a step back and looked at the bigger picture. I kept asking myself what was needed and after hundreds of hours of research, realized it wasn't available.

Taking my personal experience, my work background of corporate leadership, all the hours of research, talking to and helping thousands of parents and other addicts on what they wish their parents had done, I designed a company to fulfill the needs of the parents.

After reading all of this, you may have more questions and want to talk to someone. That's why I'm offering the opportunity for us to have a phone call. But – and this is a big one – it's only for people who are willing to truly start helping their child through addiction. If you are ready to actually change, this gift is for you. If you are truly sick and tired AND you are willing to work on yourself, it might be worth your time to start the process of supporting yourself and your loved one out of this nightmare. It's worth it for me to offer this gift if you are ready to:

- Face yourself and your denial

- Invest in your loved one's future and not support their addiction

- Allow the addict their consequences because you believe in them.

- You are willing to start setting and defending your boundaries

- Let go of your own guilt and shame that allows the addict to manipulate you.

You can choose to get your free next step strategy call. In your free strategy session with me, you will learn more about how you can truly help your loved one in addiction and what direction you should go in while also learning what else you can do to support your loved one.

In the strategy session, we will go into depth about my proven F.A.C.T.S.™ System and different ways to implement this support system into your life.

The F.A.C.T.S.™ System approaches that question for family members of "What can I do?"

There is so much lying and manipulation that happens with substance abuse, it can be hard to see the facts that are right in front of your face anymore. You don't know what to believe, you may have a hard time trusting yourself, trusting the addict, trusting doctors, therapists, etc. It's important to focus on the facts again. And F.A.C.T.S.™ stands for

Face Reality

Assess Your Situation

Commit to Yourself

Think->Respond

Show Love

Throughout this system, there are different strategies customized for you and your needs and goals. Most importantly, the strategies need to be designed around YOUR foundation you have with your child. There is no one that knows your child better than you do.

Supporting your loved one through this has to be done your way while using strategies you feel good about.

I work with people individually to start building your support system while using YOUR foundation. No parent should be asked to do something they don't agree with. So, we build off of the things you agree with.

Chapter 20:

Your Life Will Never Be the Same. The Closing Chapter and the Start of a New Life.

I want to congratulate you. You made it through this book. It was hard at times I know. I wrote it intentionally to be raw, real, and challenging, but nothing like what you face every day with your loved one.

You probably felt overwhelmed, pissed off at times. You may have even dismissed several things I said in the book and are ready to sign up for that strategy call just so you can cuss me out.

People generally either want to hug me or hit me and sometimes a little of both, but here is the thing about those feelings you are experiencing, you have to be willing to face every last one of them and dive deep because they are telling you something about yourself and the things you are dealing with internally.

Many times, people write books like this to provide inspiration and hope. And you are left with some warm fuzzies and feeling like you aren't alone through this and things are looking up for you. And then what happens, nothing actually changes and those warm fuzzies are but a distant memory as the chaos and destruction continue.

Inspiration and empowerment are two different things. Empowerment isn't about warm fuzzies. Empowerment is about taking that grounded approach that leaves you with feeling confident that you can handle anything. It is about strengthening your core, so you don't feel desperate, isolated and scared. It's about taking back control over your life.

And in order to empower yourself, you first have to look at where you give your power away. And that can be a complicated and messy process that doesn't always feel good but is necessary.

I wanted to deliver you the different ways and knowledge for you to make some real changes in your life and be able to get your power back. By doing so, I had to let you be angry with me and be willing to face that not everyone will make it all the way through this book.

Some will have put it down early on because they were looking for inspiration and figured out really quick, this was not that kind of book, and they will continue to stay in the same vicious cycles they are in.

Some people will have gotten almost all the way through the book and decided they had enough of my "bullshit" and put it down angrily because they couldn't handle it anymore and they cut themselves short, as they do many times in their life.

They don't stick with it, and miss the best part, the part that would make all the difference in the world, the end. And they stay stuck in the vicious cycle.

Many will put the book down because they felt like I spent too much time blaming them, even though I never did but they thought I was because they blame themselves without remembering this isn't about who to blame, it's about what you can do.

But you, you should congratulate yourself on making it through because that means you have a fighting chance of breaking the vicious cycle you are in and coming out the other side. You are giving yourself the chance to get back and heal the relationship you have with your loved one. You are one of the few that is willing to do what it's going to take to get through this.

This book is meant to splinter and plant seeds in your brain that will blossom as time goes on. In the best way, you have no idea the amount of hope and light at the end of the tunnel you have given yourself.

Gaining confidence in yourself is really about being aware of where you aren't confident and removing the belief systems that aren't serving you, and gaining that confidence in yourself again will support you investing in your son/daughter to help get them out of this alive and become the person you know they can be.

Congratulations. You are given the opportunity to shape your life, and therefore shape the life you have with your child. And the biggest support and help you can give them and you is to take me up on my offer for a next step strategy call, because the journey continues.

"We all make mistakes, have struggles, and even regret things in our past. But you are not your mistakes, you are not your struggles, and you are here NOW with the power to shape your day and your future."

— **Steve Maraboli,**

Certificate:

*Limited Offer:
Request a
FREE
Next Step Strategy
Session

Jennifer Maneely invites you or one family member to a private consultation.

To register go to
www.schedulewithjen.com

If asked for a promo code, please use "book"

*The offer is open to all purchasers of this book. Original proof of purchase is required. The offer is limited to limited to qualified individuals and availability of time in the schedule as deemed by Jennifer Maneely. Jennifer Maneely reserves the right to refuse consultation to anyone it believes does not qualify. This is a limited time offer and must be completed by the date shown on the website of www.maneelyconsulting.com. The value of this FREE consultation for you or a family member is $350 as of time printed. Participant in the consultations are under no additional financial obligation whatsoever to Maneely Consulting, Inc. or Jennifer Maneely. Free consultation not redeemable for cash. Jennifer Maneely reserves the right to discontinue this Limited Offer at any time.

ABOUT THE AUTHOR

 **Jennifer Maneely,** a recovering addict with over a decade clean, had an epiphany while working for a leadership development company. A large percentage of their clients were desperately struggling with how to handle adult kids in addiction. Because of her hard-won experience in addiction, she helped them by providing education, developing strategies, and providing the empowering messages they needed. Their loved ones often started getting better. Jen recognized that her insights into addiction world coupled with her experience as a coach, called her to serve at a higher level and she started her own company. She now dedicates herself full-time to helping parents that have loved ones with substance abuse issues. She has helped thousands of parents and other recovering addicts, and she can help you.

SERVICES:

Self-Directed: Many parents often find themselves not ready to reach out and talk to people about their lives but have a desire to get help with their loved one. For parents that wish to keep their private lives private, Jen has put together an online program that goes through in detail about the F.A.C.T.S.™ System. The program is only for parents that are ready to make some real changes to their situation.

www.thefactssystem.com

One-on-One: Parents who are ready to dive deep into understanding their dynamics and learn how to implement the F.A.C.T.S.™ System into their foundation on a more personal level, they can receive personal development coaching.

Speaking Engagements: Jen enjoys sharing her message of hope and collaborates with groups of people that have a desire to develop strategies surrounding the overwhelming problem of addiction our society is facing. She goes to schools, churches, corporations, and other organizations that have a desire to make real change in the world of addiction.

Contact Jennifer Maneely

Email: Jennifer@ManeelyConsulting.com

Or you can go to www.Schedulewithjen.com to set an appointment.

10197662R10072

Made in the USA
Monee, IL
26 August 2019